Words of Truth, Hope, Peace, and Love

Alfred Fico

iUniverse, Inc.
Bloomington

Words of Truth, Hope, Peace, and Love

Copyright © 2011 Alfred Fico

All rights reserved. No part of this book may be used or reproduced by any means, graphic, electronic, or mechanical, including photocopying, recording, taping or by any information storage retrieval system without the written permission of the publisher except in the case of brief quotations embodied in critical articles and reviews.

iUniverse books may be ordered through booksellers or by contacting:

iUniverse
1663 Liberty Drive
Bloomington, IN 47403
www.iuniverse.com
1-800-Authors (1-800-288-4677)

Because of the dynamic nature of the Internet, any Web addresses or links contained in this book may have changed since publication and may no longer be valid. The views expressed in this work are solely those of the author and do not necessarily reflect the views of the publisher, and the publisher hereby disclaims any responsibility for them.

Any people depicted in stock imagery provided by Thinkstock are models, and such images are being used for illustrative purposes only.

Certain stock imagery © Thinkstock.

ISBN: 978-1-4502-8154-6 (pbk)
ISBN: 978-1-4502-8155-3 (ebk)

Library of Congress Control Number: 2010918927

Printed in the United States of America

iUniverse rev. date: 1/18/2011

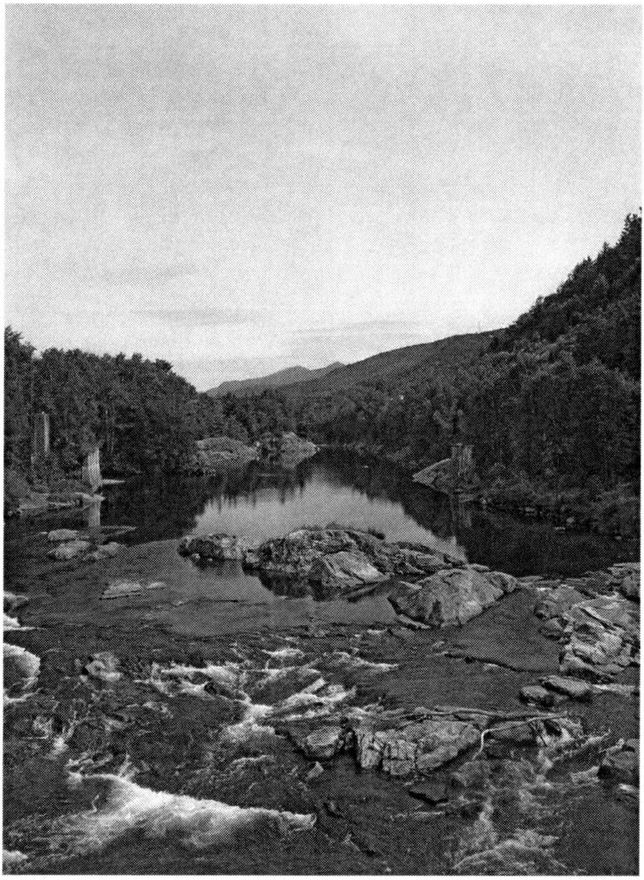

Acknowledgments

I would like to thank and dedicate this book to Jesus. He died for you and me and remains waiting for us at the right hand of the Father up in the sky.

I know I shall never be perfect, but praise the Lord of Lords and King of Kings for the ultimate loving sacrifice He has graciously gifted to me by laying His son down to die for all my sins.

I know Jesus shall always be there for us because I have witnessed so many wonderful miracles that can only be proven by God's loving mercy.

I can't thank You, my loving Father, enough for all You have done for me and those in my life: my family, friends, and especially, my church family.

The love, mercy, grace, and power from Your Holy Spirit that we have from You in our congregation is so undeserved that we all humbly bow down before You in love, knowing there's no other way to live and love others but by the way You have shown us *love*.

I humbly decrease as You graciously increase in my soul.

I pray that this book brings lost souls to You and that they are saved.

This gift I have undeservingly received from You, Lord, is to further Your kingdom.

You created and we destroyed. May the world come to You, our Savior, and may we all change our earthly behavior.

I give special thanks to one of my best friends, Jerry Tirico, for all of the photos in my book.

Humbly His Forever,

Alfred Fico Jr.

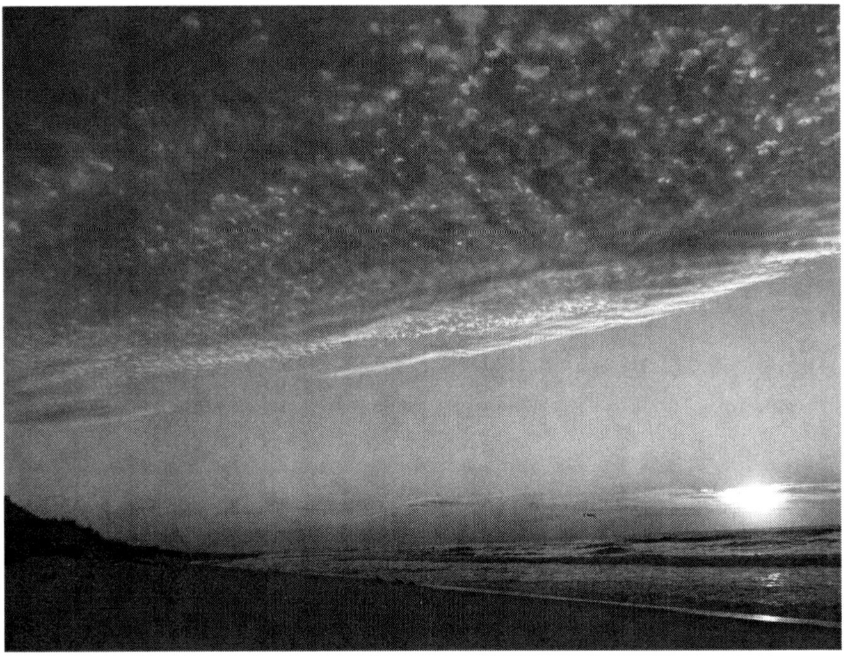

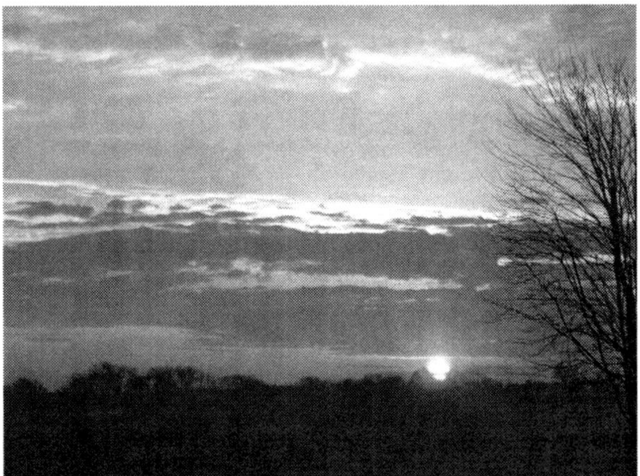

A Day in My Life He Shines So Perfectly

I wake up lying in bed, praising God for this wonderful day;
On the way to work, I see a bad accident and begin to pray.

Cars are upside down, totaled and blazing on fire:
I know this isn't an act from the God of my heart's desire.
In my office, I see people looking so hopeless and down;
I sing in my heart, praising Jesus for joy and His crown.

My first client comes in seeming angry and annoyed.
He doesn't have the love of Jesus; this is definitely his void.

I get through some appointments till I get to the last one;
I am relieved when we meet because they, too, love Jesus, God's son.

I leave the office and enter the parking lot: what do I see?
A man with one shoe, a torn shirt, asking me for money.

With my God-loving heart, I give him what's in my pocket joyfully;
Walking to my car, I turn around, and he has vanished mysteriously.

Driving home, the rain's so bad I have to pull over, and what do I see?
The same one-shoe man trying to stay dry under a tree.

I flash my lights and beep my horn so he recognizes it's me.
He asks if I can drop him off at the diner when the rain stops completely.

As we're driving there, he tells me how God provides for everyone;
He walks into the diner, snaps his fingers, and out comes a bright sun.

I walk in the door, hearing my blessed family singing joyfully;
In the living room, I sit on the couch, about to eat my dinner and watch TV.

Only one child left that accident with minor cuts, I saw on the news that night;
I go to my children's room and fall asleep holding them tight.

I pray before I fall asleep for all who don't love Jesus the way I do,
Knowing His hope is the only way to get through, as the man I met knew.

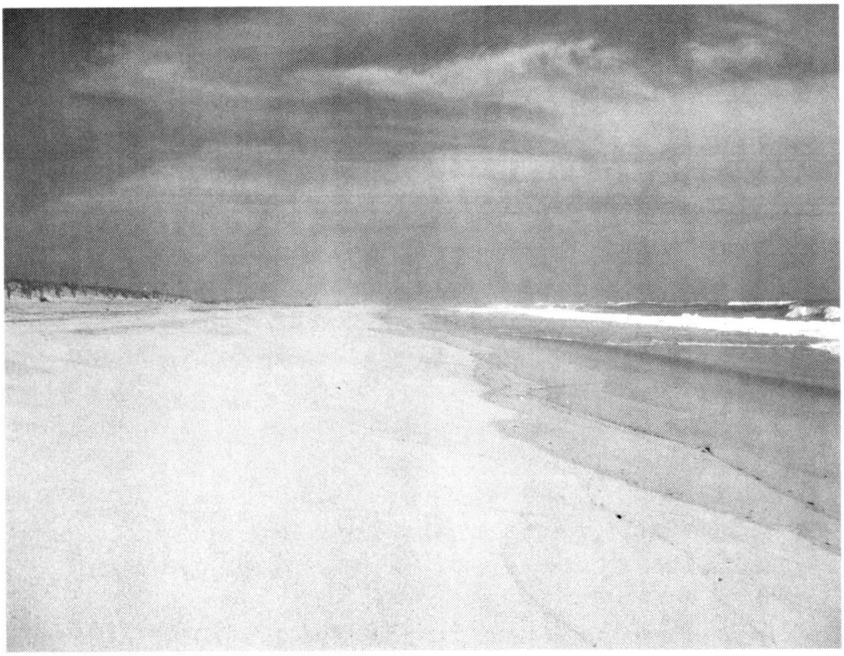

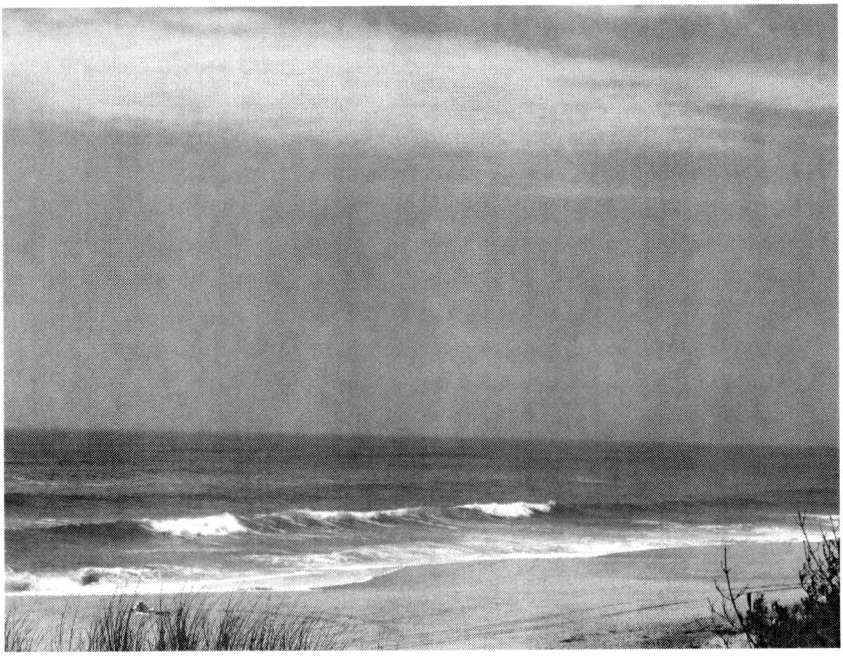

An Honorable Dedication Service

Service was filled strongly with the Holy Spirit today;
Once worship started, you felt Him each and every way.

Elizabeth Lanni sang a beautiful gospel song;
With her voice so perfect, not a thing sounded wrong.

It was a moving beat, and everyone got up and clapped;
Even the babies were dancing once they got off their parents' laps.

Alyssa Esposito got up—a true miracle how her heart was healed.
She thanked Pastor Dominick for being there through her ordeal.

Joel Ernst and his family spoke of how you touch their lives;
Somehow, all the love our families have for you all truly jives.

Letters from Gabe and Dominica: how grateful they are;
You are obviously wonderful parents by far.

Miss Ruth got up and told us what P-A-S-T-O-R meant when she spoke;
Most of it was grateful, deep, and loving, but she threw in a joke.

Michael wrote a letter: the pastor was always there, praying over him;
He was run over by a bus, and life had seemed very dim.

One of my favorites was a blessed human video by Stacy, the troublemaker.
The song was called "Yes" and for many became a tear-taker.

Your life is a true example that the fruit of your mom lives on;
In this church, we love each other; it's truly a rare bond.

Pastor Dominick and Kathie, your lives you gave to serve our Lord.
I have no doubt in heaven you both shall receive such a great reward.

When I bring new friends into church for service on Sunday,
They feel the Holy Spirit, so maybe to return this, I strongly pray.

Our God has blessed this congregation with His strong, undying love;
One reason is that both of your hearts are as gentle as doves.

I thank God every day for you both teaching me
The correct way to love and how a Christian should be.

I have my own spin on what the title "pastor" stands for,
So I'm writing my next poem kind of like Miss Ruth said before.

Blessed

Be thankful, for the Lord is great;
Let Him rule your hearts, and do not ever hate.
Everyone shall experience trouble here on earth.
Seek God for shelter; He knows what your life is worth.
Sending Jesus to die on the cross washed all our sins clean;
Even for the worst of sinners, Jesus intervened.
Days are numbered, and only God knows when Jesus again shall be seen.

Humble

He saved us by letting His son viciously die—
Ultimate display of love for our sins was the reason why.
Many gathered to see Him nailed to the cross,
Believing why He died was far from our loss.
Loving us so deeply, even though we didn't deserve,
Eternal life is what He gave us, so Lord, I am here to forever serve.

Peace

Pray for all things, no matter how bad it seems;
Everyone goes through rough water, but He redeems.
Allow Jesus to overflow your heart with His precious love;
Christ brings nothing less than the tenderness of a pure white dove.
Enter into His arms and feel the ***peace*** that can only come from above.

Faith

Fear not what we cannot see;
Allow the Lord to reveal what shall be.
In times of trouble, run to Jesus; He'll set us free.
There is a god who deeply loves you and me;
Have *faith* that Jesus shall always rescue thee.

Calvary Poem

Waves and darkness, rain and storms:
My Lord, Your love always performs.

In the deepest of valleys or on the highest mountain,
Your living waters flow through my heart like a fountain.

Your peace and joy I pray we all receive from the Holy Spirit;
I want to run down the streets with praise and cheer it.

I'm so deeply in love with our Lord and Savior;
I pray for His mercy at the pearly gates for my life's behavior.

I can never repay You for Your son's display;
I am sorry for my sins, and it hurts when I disobey.

I know You allow us to fall and stumble;
It's Your perfect way of keeping us humble.

The depth of Your love we shall never understand;
When Jesus rose, they knew He was at the Father's right hand.

Who else would let their son die crucified on the cross?
No earthly father would survive such a great loss.

So when you think things are going bad, don't stay sad;
Instead, praise the Lord for the blood of the Lamb and be glad.

Hanging on the cross till His very last breath was God's son,
Saying, "Forgive them, Father, for they not know what they have done."

Thank you, dear Lord, for all that You've done.
I can't put in words what You did through Your son.

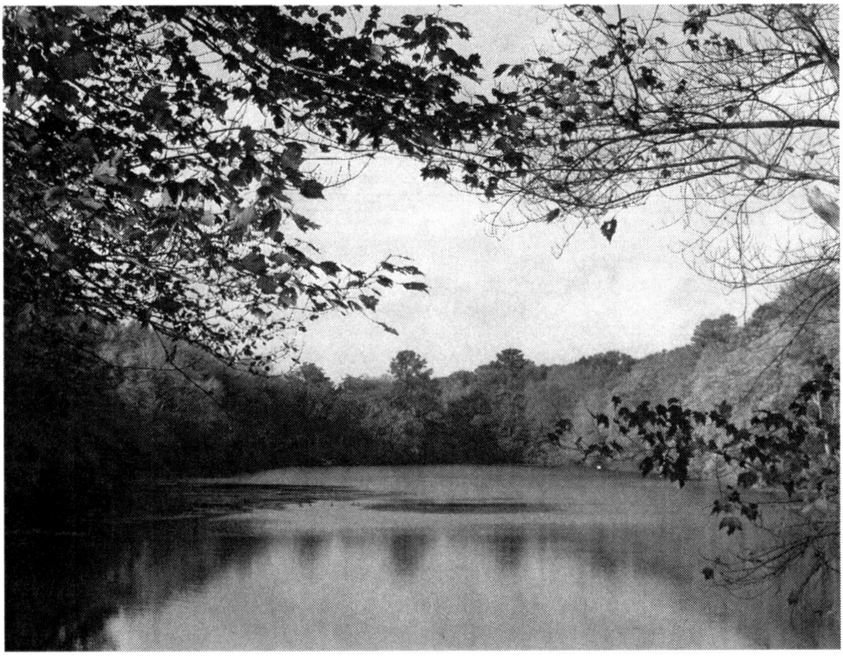

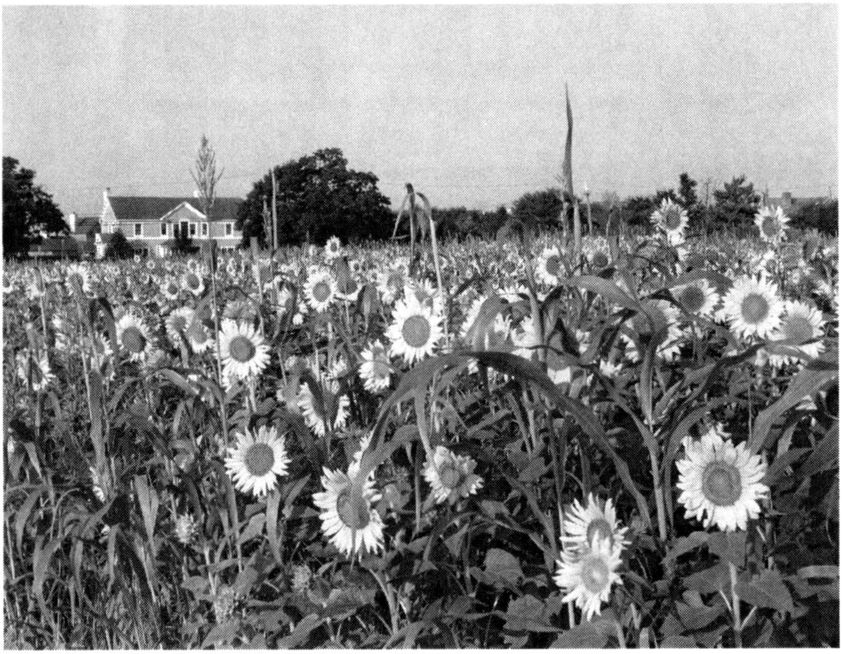

A Service to One Beautiful Christian Woman

Service started off with great worship and praise;
The Holy Spirit had me in awe and amazed.

The last song was my favorite, called "Revelation";
It was deep and had my tears flowing without hesitation.

Pastor Dominick began service with receiving communion;
We all agreed, ate His body, and drank His blood in union.

He then began reading from the Bible version of King James;
I smiled because it's the one I have, so the words are the same.

The woman I am writing about, named Doris Scibetta:
What an awesome Christian woman—wish I would have met her.

She served our Lord with such deep passion and love;
She is at peace, dancing and looking down from above.

The pastor shared a story about how she hid their money;
The spots you wouldn't expect, but we all found it funny.

He then began to tell us how she sang to his dad every night;
I am sure their marriage was so blessed, and they both slept tight.

Doris touched so many lives, and her fruit continues to save;
Her legacy shall live on as the way a good Christian should behave.

I know how blessed so many lives are because of you,
Especially when I hear your son preach and know I'm one of them too.

Mrs. Scibetta, we all agree you're enjoying God's peace up in heaven;
If God rated your life from one to ten, I bet he would give you an eleven.

In loving memory of Doris Scibetta.

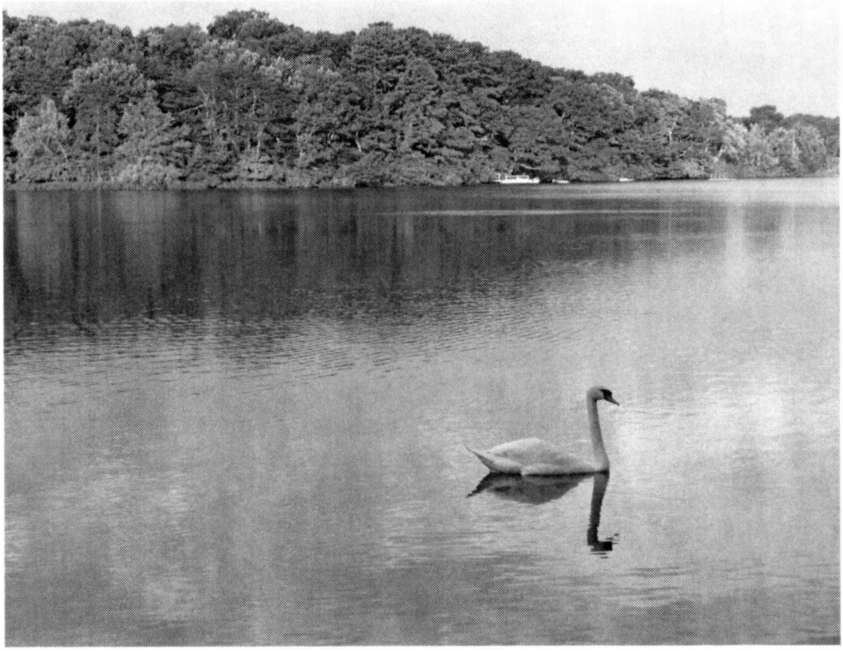

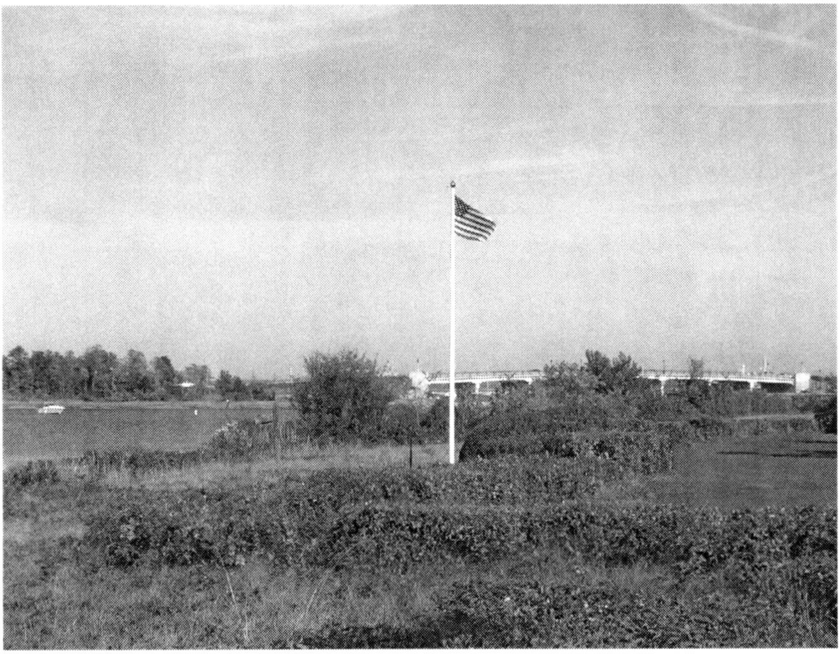

Double Portion of Love with a Side of Freedom

Worship began with some awesome song;
All our hearts felt this is where we belong.

We felt God's presence with tender hearts;
His love is so deep; weeping was just the start.

The service was packed with so many hands raised;
I knew this service was going to put our hearts in a daze.

The pastor was so overwhelmed with God's holy love,
He stopped the worship, which was a sign from above.

We received communion with true thanks to our Savior,
We know what He wants is our hearts and good behavior.

I heard an usher say he ran out of communion;
This made me feel many Christians came to service in union.

Freedom and love were the calling on every soul in His place;
I found myself with a river of tears flowing down my face.

The Holy Spirit gave the pastor a great message and word;
All hearts were given His hope once we had heard.

Pat spoke in tongues, and then Risa got up to translate;
It was the presence of God as only He can communicate.

It was the Holy Spirit; neither of them planned what to say.
God has His word come to us in only a father's perfect way.

The depth of His love we shall never understand;
We have freedom once we allow our hearts in His hands.

I closed my eyes in deep worship as I felt my soul leave;
It was Jesus: I flew with a feeling only He can make me receive.

I can feel God blessing us as our congregation keeps growing;
I know others will flock and our school attendance shall be overflowing!

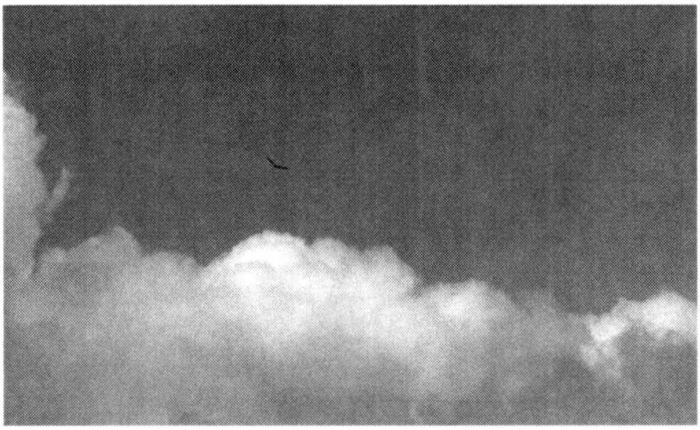

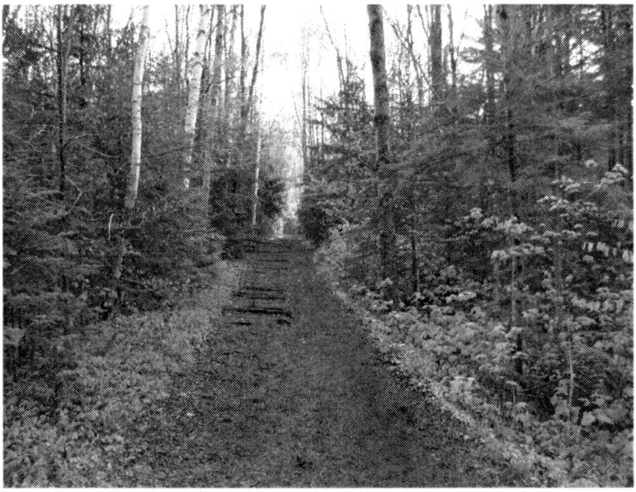

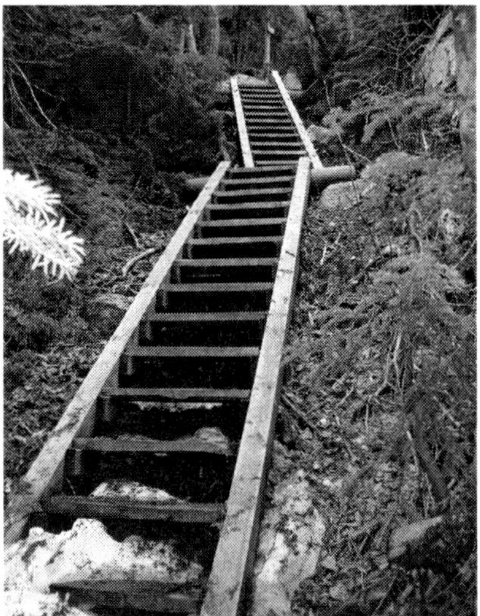

Finding God's Peace When He Calls Them Home!

Though our earthly flesh grieves and your soul believes,
Run into God's open arms for comfort, and feel His love your heart receives.
I know it's painful to feel joy when we lose someone close;
Only God's peace can settle your soul; He loves you the most.
When you feel alone, and your heart has an empty space,
Read your Bible, cry to Him, and feel the warmth of God's embrace.
Though sometimes on the date that they died, we feel extra sorrow,
Know God's love, peace, and joy is ours to have, not just to borrow.
Draw near to the Lord when your heart feels hurt and broken;
He knows and heals pain for the grieving before your first word is spoken.
Open your Bible and read Psalms 34:18 and Corinthians 15:51–55;
When the last trumpet is blown, our heavenly bodies shall come *alive!*
Read Thessalonians 4:13–14 of His wonderful truth about sorrow;
Jesus's return brings back Christians who've died, and this could happen tomorrow.
Though we love God on earth, life shall bring pain and suffering;
Thank you, our great almighty Lord, for sending Jesus as our buffer.
Get back into those rivers of living water flowing in your heart;
Let Jesus fill you back up and God crush that sorrow apart.
O death, where is your victory, and what happens to your sting?
My faithful, loving God conquered all these things, and hearts shall forever sing!

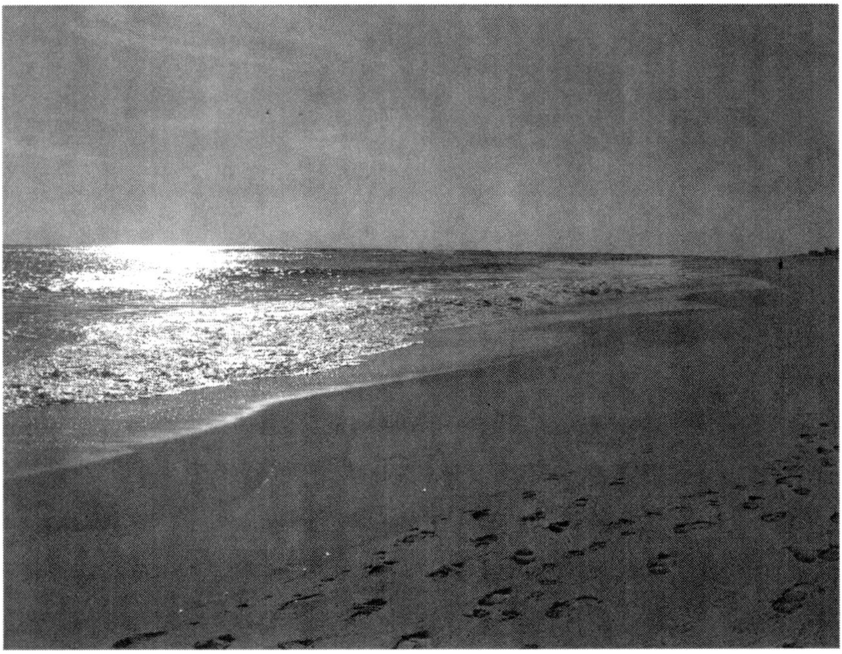

God Is So Close to Us

The Lord is near and never far;
He heals all hearts, no matter how deep your scar.

Down on your knees, you seek His face;
He comes to save souls with His love and never-ending grace.

Build up your faith in our Savior and don't fear;
God allowed Jesus to die for the sins of those He loves so dear.

Our only way into heaven was by vicious bloodshed.
Give your life to Christ; His peace covers you while lying in bed.

Wake up each day praising Him, first in your heart;
You win with God's armor against those trying to tear you apart.

When you are in the midst of life's worst storm, and it feels like hell,
Cry out—He hears you, and your heart shall be renewed, singing it is well.

So keep God's love under lock and key;
When the evil one attacks, you shall win and watch him flee.

Your relationship with God is never idled; it's drawing near or pushing away,
So run to Him because He loves you, no matter how far you stray.

He's waiting for you with open arms and a loving heart;
Forever, He's right next to you, right from the very start. *Amen!*

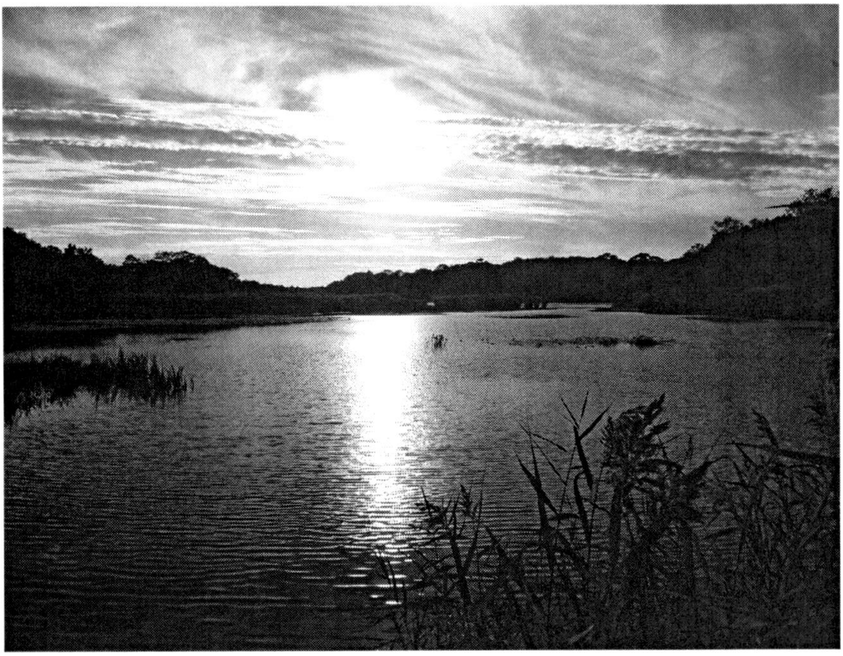

God's Miracle Baby, Jayden

Marc, Melissa, and Jayden: what a special family of three.
Lord, bless this child and his parents; I beg for Your mercy.
In my life, I have seen Jesus heal so many before;
Please, dear God, I cry to You for Jayden to be one more.
My heart is Yours, God, to give praise for this miracle baby;
Let this be a witness to all: here and forever, keep them under Your safety.
I know this world is filled with pain, suffering, and worry.
Take hold; Jesus shall win and prevail healing for Jayden in a hurry.
God has given such blessings in our lives that we can never repay;
That's why every night, I cry on my knees to God and pray.
Nothing is more powerful than the love of God on earth;
Jayden we receive as a miracle and gift from Jesus right at birth.
We are never born perfect, and life may bring us storms;
Run into Jesus's open arms and watch the miracles He performs.
Today, we sing in our hearts and pray for Jayden to be healed;
Praying this brings you three closer to God to see His love here revealed.
Pray to God all day long, asking Him for protection over you all;
Think how strong you can become when Jesus hears your crying call.
Speak about how big your God is over life's difficult situations;
He cares for us when we give Him our hearts without hesitations.
I love and pray for God's peace over your special family forever!

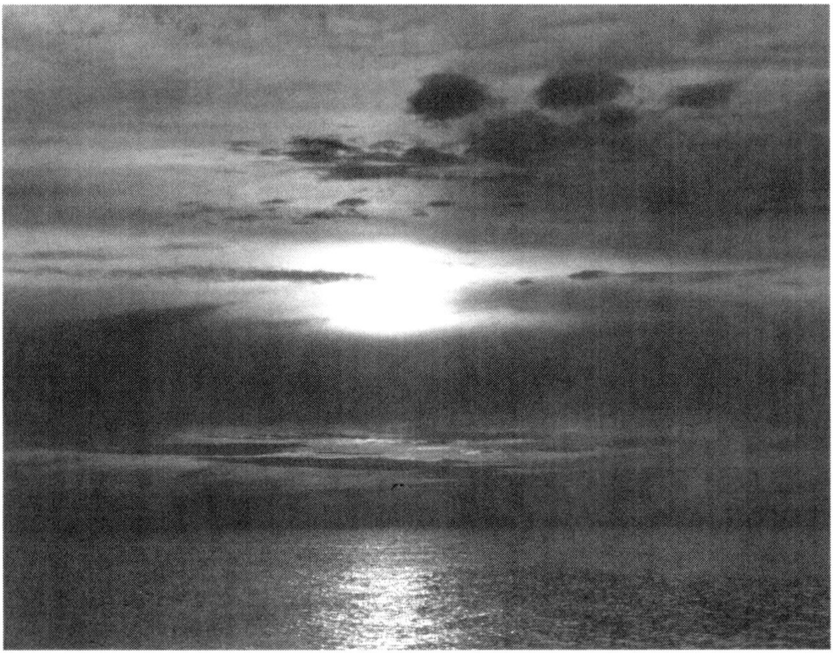

Grace

Grace is undeserved, kind, and lasts forever;
If it were not from God, heaven would be never.

Grace can never be earned;
If God didn't grant it, we'd all be burned.

All our great works cannot get us into heaven;
Amen! For God's grace, we can enter at any time, just like a 7-Eleven.

Grace can be abused; people think it's a license to sin.
If we purposely live this way, nothing godly shall come in the end.

So please, pray for yourself and others too.
Then thank God there's enough grace for me and you.

So shout and praise for God's great grace;
Show Him your love and bow down your face.

His grace covers all the wrong we have done;
His immeasurable love was displayed in the horrific death of His son.

Grace shall cover all sins, no matter how badly you were wrong;
It's a gift from God, knowing that in your heart is where He belongs.

Receiving grace was the only way we have been saved;
Do your best by showing the world how Christians should behave.

So, I humbly say this that you may share it with those still lost;
God let His son die, and the grace we receive was such a high cost.

GRACE: God Rescues All Christians Eternally!

Happy Father's Day, God

I am thankful for the immeasurable and undeserved love;
Heavenly Father, Your grace fits my soul like a perfect glove.

I cannot repay the love You placed upon my heart;
You took me in your arms, even though my world had fallen apart.

I can't put into words the sacrifices You have made for me;
Though life has its roughest storms, Your love lets me rest peacefully.

Oh how He loves us, and He is my daddy's Father as well;
Forever in my heart, oh dear Lord, is where you shall eternally dwell.

We won't ever understand a love such as this one,
Especially when You allowed the brutal murder of Your son.

I celebrate Father's Day for the two men who mean the most:
My earthly dad and heavenly Father, whose work I love to boast.

So when you feel lonely, like you have lost your way,
Keep praying and have faith in Him each and every day.

My Father, You alone are everything I am ever going to need;
I am so gratefully humble for how You sat back and let Your son bleed.

Be joyful in the Lord's loving peace if your dad is no longer here,
For it is written there's no sorrow in heaven nor does anyone shed a tear.

Happy Father's Day to You, God, and to you, my earthly dad! **Humbly His Forever, Fred Jr.**

His Sweet Peace That Makes the Soul Salivate

His peace puts your soul in such a calm place;
I must thank Him every night, bowing down my face.

God offers us forgiveness for all our sins;
This is where your soul's healing begins.

No matter how bad it gets in your raging storm,
There's a peace He gives and makes your heart feel warm.

It might look so bad with a report that's financial;
Fear not, for in His arms, the peace is more than substantial.

You may have been told your job soon may be ending;
Be strong, have faith in Jesus, for a new miracle He is sending.

Winds may be swirling and waves may seem violent;
Praise the Lord, for He brings sweet peace and makes it all silent.

We may feel there's no way out and everyone has left our side;
With the blink of an eye, His spirit shows signs He shall provide.

Once your heart surrenders all to His *mighty* love,
The peace begins to fit your soul like a perfect glove.

Nothing is better than praying to God for His peace over every situation;
His love, mercy, hope, and son's sacrifice was done without hesitation.

So never turn from God, no matter how bad life seems;
He shall turn your nightmares into heavenly dreams.

At night before you sleep, use these words while you're praying:
"Lord, please always let Your peace keep my soul from straying."

Life Is Too Short, So Live in His Joy

Life is too short to wake up and begin any day with a single regret;
At night when you lie down, count your blessings so you don't forget.
Always pray for those people who treat you right and treat you wrong;
When you do this, God knows your heart is right where it belongs.
Don't waste your energy on being angry or hating someone;
Show Jesus's love today because tomorrow, you might not see the sun.
Tomorrow's not promised, so be a blessing to someone today;
You may be keeping someone's heart from going astray.
We are only here for a short time and need to share His great news:
What peace and joy we can receive, if living for Jesus is what we choose.
Live in God's unspeakable joy as souls rejoice from His loving heart;
If your choice is anything different, your short life shall always be torn apart.
Why not enjoy the blessings and gifts God has planned for you and me?
This life is short, and when we find His peace, there's no better high.
Be not wasteful of the time you spend here before we die;
Enjoy all that God has to offer us—you could be gone in the blink of an eye.

Marriage Till We Go Home

Marriage is supposed to be blissful, and yet so many divorce;
This is far from God's plan, yet perfect for Satan's course.

Please conquer this with God's love in your heart, or it shall be your loss;
After all, Jesus died for your sins and carried *your cross!*

So, when you argue over meaningless earthly things,
Run as one to our Father for a look at the sacrifice and love He brings.

You vow to be as one in God's house and forever in His eyes;
The pain a marriage could bring is well worth God's heavenly prize.

So, when you feel as if all hope in your marriage is forever lost,
Together on your knees, thank Jesus for the brutal death your lives had cost.

Take it all to the cross where Jesus brutally died,
Knowing boldly you shall never be denied.

When it looks like nothing is going right and it's all falling apart,
Remember only God, your Father, can mend your broken heart.

Draw closer to Him lovingly together, united as one;
The storms shall vanish, and your love returns as bright as the morning sun.

Don't think divorce is the only answer to all the problems of marriage;
If you both focus on God's love, every year shall be greater than average.

So, before you say harsh words to each other that may stain the heart,
Think before you speak them; it's one of the best ways to start.

Show love and appreciation each and every day; that's God's only way.
The marriage shall triumph over all storms, and your hearts shall never decay.

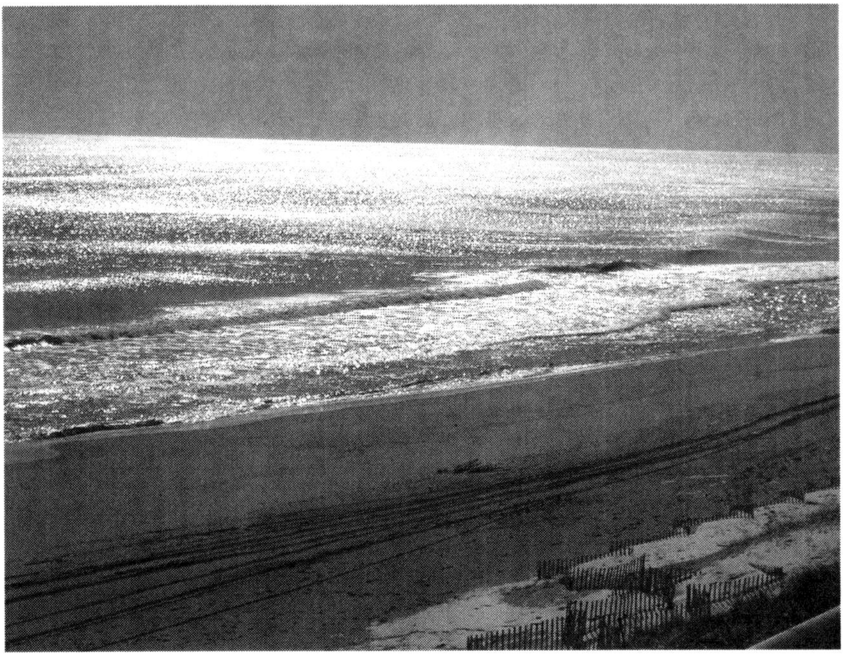

Pastor's Appreciation Poem

P is for *passion:*

When the pastor preaches, I feel his hungry *passion* for God's great love.
It makes me weep from how deeply the Holy Spirit comes down from above.

A stands for *anointed:*

The love in Center Moriches house of God is truly *anointed.*
Being a pastor takes great sacrifice; only few are appointed.

S is for *strength:*

The *strength* of a pastor must hold the body of Christ together.
Though hard at times, God's strength triumphs over any weather.

T means *teacher* and *tender:*

A pastor must have a *tender* heart and *teach* kindness to all.
He must sit back and not be harsh but be there when things fall.

O is for *overtime:*

His hours are long—now home and the workday is finished;
Overtime kicks in as the phone rings and family time is diminished.

R is for *renew:*

A pastor must keep our hearts fresh, excited, and *renewed.*
If he doesn't change things sometimes, then we won't have a packed pew.

Pastor Dominick, you are one of the most humble men I know;
When people look at how you live your life, it is only God you show.

Your hunger for truth and the rawness of God's word:
There's nothing sugar coated when your voice is to be heard.

I see you walk extra carefully and fear God more than most;
Sundays, my soul awakens in joy for His truth of knowledge you're going to boast.

Behind our blessed pastor is God's love pouring from his dearest wife;
Kathie, I must say you're a fine example of how to live a Christian life.

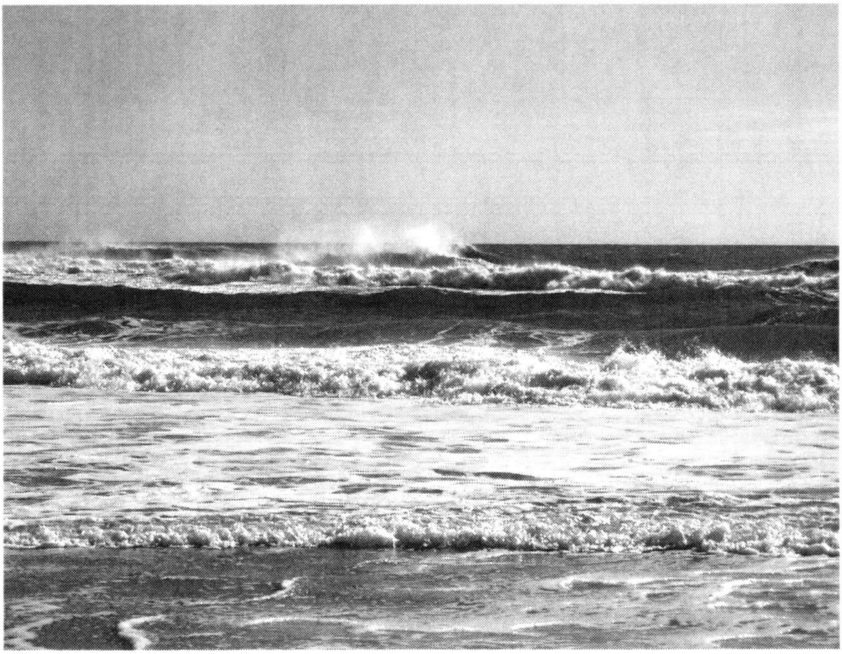

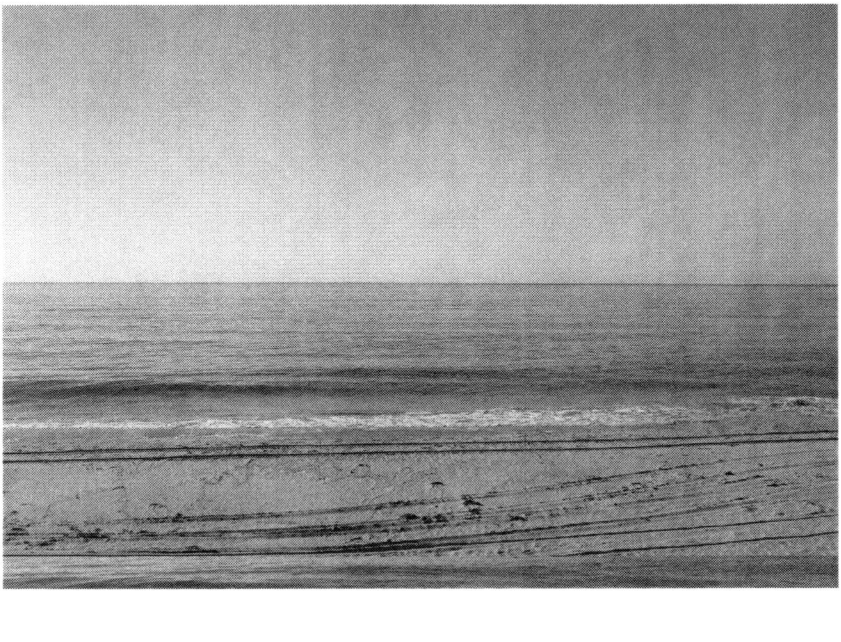

Protection and Hope in All Storms

Stand in the rain and run to God to remove all the pain.
The Creator, our Lord, shall make the sun shine, and joy shall remain.
No matter how deep and windy your storm can be,
Jesus died for all sins and sufferings, so you can be set free.
Time is short here, and we all experience trouble on earth;
God allowed Jesus to die for us; that is how much we are worth.
Take refuge in our almighty Savior, no matter what life may bring.
God shall carry you through it all until your heart can joyfully sing.
When you're sitting alone and feeling as if your life is dark,
Kneel and pray with a tender heart, and God shall save you like Noah's ark.
No matter how deep your ocean seems and how huge are the waves that crash,
We have the Mighty One, our God, to remove all the sufferings in a flash!
Life may seem so bad in the midst of our biggest downward slope;
Imagine not loving Jesus or feeling the presence of His great hope.
When everything falls apart, and the swirling winds are so violent,
Trust in the Lord who created heaven and earth, for He shall make them silent.
Truth be told that Jesus came to earth for us as God in human form:
Every day, I praise His holy name, thankful none of us experienced His storm.

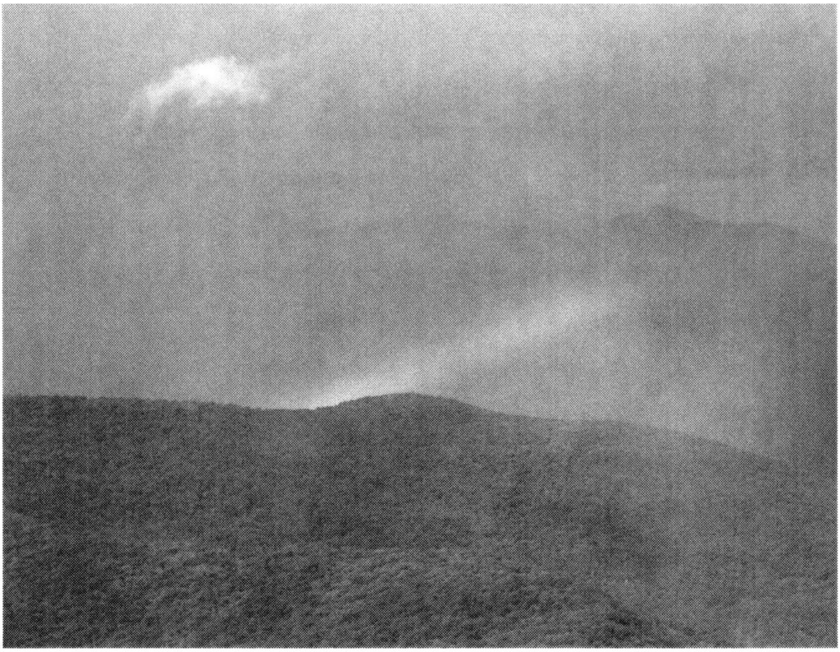

Resurrection Poem

Everyone thinks it's about some silly bunny,
Searching for colored eggs, and acting real funny.

The world doesn't know about the *true* meaning of Easter—what a shame:
How Jesus died brutally to save your soul, and we are to blame.

Instead of Easter, we should call it "the Resurrection,"
So we humbly sit in silence, thinking about God's perfection.

It's a shame how some attend service Easter and Christmas only;
If they came all year, they wouldn't feel so hopeless and lonely.

He died on a Thursday, nailed to the cross;
If it were not for Jesus, this world would be at a loss.

Three days later, His tomb was found empty;
God's proven to me that His grace is more than plenty.

Christians, this is the holiest day for you and I;
There's nothing like praising our Lord with hands held to the sky.

This is the *truth* of an amazing love story,
How He died for us so we may enter His kingdom in glory.

So when it feels like everything in life is falling apart,
Know that Jesus died for us, and He shall protect your heart.

This day shall bring us hope, peace, and joy, deep inside;
Please share this *truth* so the world knows Jesus shall provide.

Today, we celebrate our Savior's son has *risen!*
Praise Lord God for making *all* our sins forgiven.

Resurrection Service

For Christians, the holiest day had begun;
My heart had such joy with many songs to be sung.

My sister had called, asking me to save her a seat;
My heart smiled, thinking of her at service: what a treat.

When I walked through His doors, I felt His love,
A feeling that can only come from up above.

This was no Easter service I had ever felt before;
I knew the Holy Spirit had something special in store.

I turned and saw my sister with my nephew, Dylan;
Now, my heart was pouring over with such a thrill in.

I held him as we worshipped, singing and clappin';
He had an idea about the joy that had happened.

The pastor spoke of what a savior we have in Jesus—
The words of peace that only He can please us.

He brought His son to earth as a sacrifice to die;
If not, eternity wouldn't be an option for you and me.

The death and torture He went through was so severe;
Every time I think how deeply He loves us, I start to tear.

The things He did for us so that we may have salvation:
I know that God is our portion forever, with no hesitation.

Amen, our Jesus has overcome death, and the third day He was raised;
I forever give Him my whole heart and every breath to Him I praise.

We shall never know the measure of God's love;
When I think of what He has done, I feel Him shine from above.

The sermon was over, and at His altar, we joined hands in songs of praise;
I held my buddy in my arms and saw his hands raised.

Seeing this made tears of joy run down my face.
His altar with my church family on earth: there is no better place.

I have a mission: Dylan is saved and gives his heart over to You.
This I pray happens soon so he can learn of all that You do.

The way You made Your son, Jesus, show His resurrection:
It was a display of Your love, grace, mercy, and perfection.

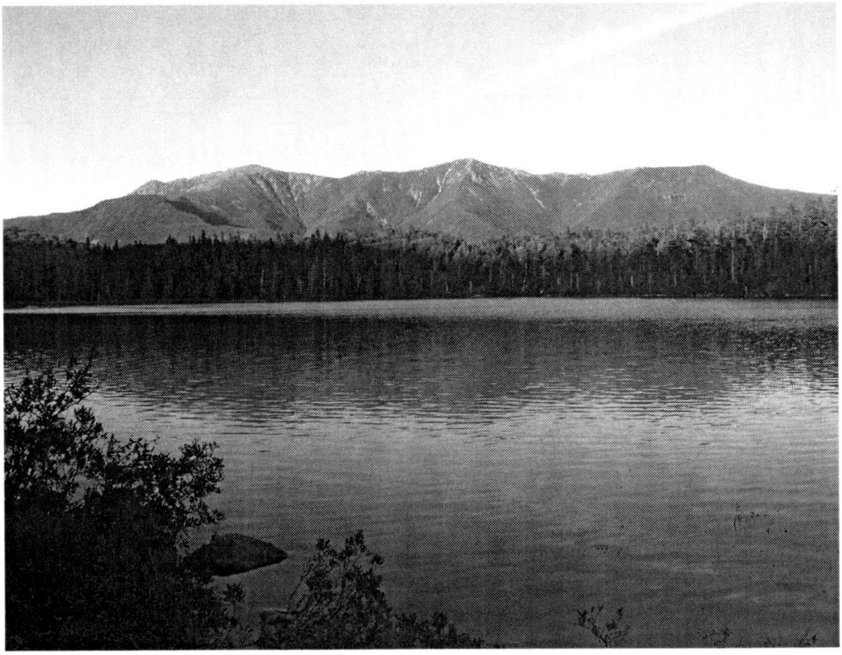

It's *All* and Always about *Jesus*

The Holy Spirit, Jesus, and God are all the same, yes, together as one;
We could never enter heaven if God hadn't become human in His son.
What our heavenly Father is doing, Jesus does as well;
We shall feel God's peace when we let Him in our hearts to dwell.
He is almighty by nature and worthy of all praise;
We must feed our souls every Sunday in song with hands raised.
We are the body of Christ and must show love to our neighbors,
Letting Him shine through us to the lost and showing them Christian behaviors.
Fix your heart, soul, and eyes directly on Jesus;
Nothing on earth compares to the way He can please us.
Knowing Jesus and loving Him: there is no greater thing;
His peace you receive is better than a perfect day in spring.
He can save the lost by us showing His love and sowing a seed;
Don't waste a chance to share with the world why Jesus had to bleed.
If you feel you're drifting, don't grow cold inside; it would be a shame.
Read your Bible, and His word shall rekindle your heart's flame.
Falling in love with Jesus is the best on earth that you ever have done;
God's love shall never leave you, proof through what He did for us with His son.
When God gives a chance to open people's hearts to receive their salvation,
Pray His love radiates through you and jump at the opportunity without hesitation.

Someone Needs You to Be a Blessing Every Day

  Someone needs you to make his or her heart and soul smile;
God shall give you the chance, but are you willing to go the extra mile?
  Why be angry at someone or something? It's so draining;
Shake it off and make someone smile if you hear him or her complaining.
  Jesus is the biggest blessing that we all need to share;
Let His light shine through you so they know you truly care.
  God wants us all to have His peace even through our worst storms;
Show God's love to a stranger: be kind and make him or her feel warm.
  Let His love and spirit radiate through your life to everyone;
Sow a seed and tell those who don't know about God and His son.
  Someone needs to be blessed today; why not be that person?
For this, God shall reward your heart with His joy, I'm most certain.
  What we do for the least of those less fortunate, we do unto the Lord;
Living in heaven without sorrow or sickness is our eternal reward.
  Someone could be an angel that may ask you for some money;
This could be God looking for your heart's reaction, which isn't so funny.
  Being a blessing is great, although you can't enter heaven just by being nice;
You must invite the Lord into your heart and Jesus, our ultimate sacrifice.
  You may bring a lost soul to accept Jesus Christ into his or her life and heart;
You might need someone to be your blessing one day when life's falling apart.

Teen Convention

We started off great until Sam's van broke down.
In minutes, God gave us favor, and we were north bound.

The owner knew we were a church group, to his knowledge,
Said he wouldn't charge us, and went to Bible college.

Off we went and later arrived at the hotel,
Made it to the first service, and felt the Holy Spirit as well.

The band was singing and thousands of kids had their hands raised;
God's presence was so strong, all anyone could do was worship and praise.

My tears came from so deep, and His joy filled my heart;
It felt like God's loving waters from my eyes at the very start.

Tony Cruz was the speaker, and Relevant Worship was the band;
The power of God was so strong that everyone got up to stand.

Tony's message was about stepping up and bringing others to be saved;
I wrote a song from this called "You Had Twenty-Four Hours to Save: How Would You Behave?"

This trip always gives me such peace and brings me closer to God;
I look forward to next year's trip as the youth agreed with a smiling nod.

The weekend was filled with a powerful portion of the Holy Spirit;
Made me feel like running down the streets of Syracuse and cheering it!

Holy Saturday came and off we were, back to traveling;
The weather was warm, and the sun was brightly shining.

All of a sudden, my van stalled out, and again, we were stuck;
It didn't look good for the red van until we got a hold of the repair truck.

Three hours later, we were driving south as good as new;
Thanks to God's grace and mercy to our prayers, we made it through.

We arrived back at church later on that night;
Resurrection Sunday was crowded and was a heavenly sight.

I pray for all the people who came to this convention
That the love of Jesus was all their hearts could mention.

Thank God for Mother's Day

Today, we need to show extra love to our mothers;
Thank God and her, or you would have no sisters or brothers.

Your mom is key to holding families close and together;
She would go through anything with you, no matter the weather.

She cooks, cleans, and has room to give you love;
Someone this special is a unique gift from God above.

Though we may not like everything for us she does,
She knows what's best, so don't her ask why or say because.

God made her soft to love, gentle but strong to hold us tight;
She is a special person and always prays for you every night.

I envy those moms who are single, teaching us right from wrong;
I believe they do a better job than us men and show us they're strong.

Some families get sad if Mom is gone, no matter how many years;
Even the biggest of us misses her and eyes well up with tears.

Through our faith and hope, though they're no longer here,
We can say, "I love you, Mom, because you and God are near."

So many times, my mom had sacrificed and gave her share away;
We had no idea the depth of her love; we just went on to play.

I can never thank God or you, Mom, for all you've done;
God, I am so blessed to be this woman's daughter or son.

I am older and realize how precious, Mom, you are to me;
I look back now in joyful tears on what you did for our family.

We sometimes feel we did wrong things to you,
When we didn't listen or tell you what was really true.

Mom, deep in my heart, next to God is where you stand;
He has blessed me when He put my life in your hand.

  Just know when I'm out in the world, grown and not with you,
Everything in my life is with respect and love: it's what you taught me to do.

  So, it's not just today that should we honor and love them all;
Tell Mom always how much you love her by prayer, text, or phone call.

  God, bless all the moms who have done the best they can;
Look how we've grown into fine women or men.

Humbly His Forever,

Fred Fico Jr.

The Underestimated Power of *Prayer*

There's an immeasurable power we have in prayer;
God's heart hears ours, and the miracles come beyond compare.

If you think your life a mess, and things are getting bad,
Prayer can clean it all up and make your heart feel so glad.

Focus and pray to God, even if life seems so deranged;
Prayer is so powerful; your life He can miraculously change.

He hears you regardless of how bad you have been;
Pray and know Jesus died for each and every sin.

He knows what your prayers are before you begin to speak;
He shall lift you up even though you feel so beaten and weak.

When a church comes together and prays for each other,
It's a miracle that He shows us for each sister and brother.

My entire life seeing my earthly father go through so much pain,
Praying and crying to God for Dad's healing was all that kept me sane.

I know we aren't supposed to worry, but our flesh does so.
Praying for this release brings peace: I have experienced it; I know.

Prayer means taking it all to the cross where Jesus brutally died,
Knowing boldly we shall never be denied, nor shall His love ever hide.

When it looks like life is so out of control and it's all falling apart,
Remember only He can heal you and mend your entire heart.

Pray even when things are great and also in the silent season;
God shall bring you through, and know Jesus died for a reason.

Here we pray with faces down, knowing we have been wrong;
He brings joy and peace when we worship Him in song.

No matter how sick a friend or family member can be,
Jesus can heal them all 100 percent—yes, completely!

The power of prayer we shall never know or come close to understand;
He shall walk forever with you in life, firmly holding your hand.